Infinite Contestation

Occasional Political Writings

Infinite Contestation

Occasional Political Writings

Saitya Brata Das

AAKAR

Infinite Contestation: *Occasional Political Writings*
Saitya Brata Das

First Published in August 2018

ISBN 978-93-5002-584-0

The publication of the book financially benefits from the University Grants Commission under the Special Assistance Program (SAP) that is granted to the Centre for English Studies, Jawaharlal Nehru University.

Published by
AAKAR BOOKS
28 E Pocket IV, Mayur Vihar Phase I
Delhi 110 091 India
aakarbooks@gmail.com

Laser Typeset at
Arpit Printographers, Delhi

Printed at
D.K. Fine Art Press, Delhi

For

The martyrs of our time whose blood is the light of the world, and the herald of the kingdom to come

Contents

Prologue

Thinking is not a detached, objective reflection about the world and existence; it also seeks to intervene in the world and transfigure existence. For mere description of reality as it exists, and mere objective knowledge of the world as it has already become, does not satisfy the thinker who thinks, and who suffers in the battlefield of forces, powers and laws. But she does not remain a suffering individual among others, forcing through the forces of the world; she also dreams the impossible dream of redemption of the unredeemed life. Thinking is, thus, inseparable from dreams as much as it emerges from the pain of unredeemed life. This dream is not a mere escape from the intolerableness of existence, nor is it the impracticable side of the active life; it is rather the hope that transfigures existence towards something like redemption. The mere endless activities of intervention amidst the forces of the world, and the mere-having-to-be constantly engaged with the conditioned negotiations with the political powers that exist, minus the dream elements that affirm life in its messianic redemption to come, is nothing else than the political nihilism that serves the hegemonic domination that are already operative in the world and which one intervenes in order to overcome it.

Therefore, the thinker who must intervene and be active in the world, among other sufferers, must constantly be aware of the political nihilism that is already operative in the world and which, in advance, wants to make futility of all her actions and interventions. Unfortunately, this political nihilism is omniscient in the world. This is seen most acutely when we see the professional social activists condemn the thinker and the philosopher as mere dreamers, as petty bourgeois beneficiaries who survive from other people's struggles, as if thinking is opposed to action, as if the dream for the redeemed world to come has to defeat all the acts that actively want to transform the world. The truth is rather that action without hope is nihilism, and negation of the present suffering without affirmation of a new world and new heaven is totalitarianism: this truth is not the "empirical" truth, not the truth that has already become manifested in the full light of the day of history; it is rather that truth which is latent and potent, as the messianic thinker Ernst Bloch would like to say, the truth that is yet "invisible". To see this invisible is the faith that the messianic thinker must affirm against the brutal forces that seek to overpower him. In this profound sense, all philosophical thinking, insofar as it seeks to overcome the given and affirm the not yet of the world, is essentially messianic thinking. Such affirmation demands the utmost courage of thinking of what is not-yet manifested in the world, for what is not-yet-manifest—if truly thought—is not mere nothingness of all being, but that nothingness which is pregnant with possibilities, and which are groaning and longing for birth.

Therefore, it is not enough of a task for a thinker to merely describe and comment and to clarify the state of affairs of the world that is present already; she must infinitely contest the given state of affairs, with all its injustices and sufferings, in the messianic-visionary light that is immanent yet darkened in the present, the possibility of a future order of the world to come; it is the order of justice which the future brings, the future whose invisibility today makes our "today" insufficient, wretched, intolerable existence. Therefore, we want to transform this "today", for there is always a "tomorrow"—a time to come, a time that remains—without which today is not a "today". This does not mean that today is vain and futile, but precisely opposite: today is the time to seize opportunities to transform the world, which only today is it possible, and in that sense, today is also the last day.

This paradox is difficult to grasp, and yet it is the very heart of a messianic thinking: today is the last day, for today—in its absolute singularity—will never return tomorrow; and yet, on the other hand, today derives its urgency and intensity from a tomorrow, from the possibility of a tomorrow, which means that today itself is not the end of the world, and that we still have time to act and think. Action and thinking to be meaningful, there must be tomorrow; but a tomorrow which is only the endless lengthening of time from today on the same line makes action and thinking senseless and hopeless: tomorrow must come, but not just as another today; it must be a new day, a new earth and a new heaven. This messianic paradox gives pregnancy to all our action and thinking that seeks to transform the world and transfigure existence. Today is the last "today"—we cannot miss the chances of today that only today offers; but, in the heat and fever of today if we were to lose sight of the light of justice that comes from the messianic future, then we end up in the political nihilism of all sorts, in the demonic manifestation of tyranny that seek to destroy the very possibility of future. We may call this nihilism a radical evil.

Included in this book are short articles that I have written on various occasions where I have sought to address directly to specific, given situations: they are, thus, "interventions" in the most obvious sense of the term—though all thinking is an intervention. Thus, I have addressed the question of caste oppression in Indian society as much as the question of sexual repression, and the most painful question in our most immediate moment:

the destruction of the university by demonic forces of our time. These articles are published in various blogs and e-magazines. I have not therefore tried to transform the texts in order to make them appear here, but let them stay as they have appeared at first, so that the reader can understand the texts as emerging out of specific situations and speaking to those situations, though the insights that appear in these articles are by no means exhausted in those situations. Insofar as these philosophical insights receive their undiminished depth from the invisible light of justice that is not yet realized in the world, they exceed all given, specific, concrete situations in order to open up that which has not yet become a *topos* in the world. This is my humble way, as a thinker, address to various nihilisms at work in today's world. Instead of abstracting eternity from its contamination with time in order to contemplate the truth of eternity in an inviolate way, the philosopher on the other hand must intensify temporality itself to apocalyptically burst itself out of all possible closures in the light of the messianic violence of eternity that must come, interrupting and yet fulfilling time.

The Price of Civilization*

Taking its point of departure from Sigmund Freud's insight in his *Civilization and its Discontent* that an immense amount of repression is the price that humanity has to pay for its civilization, this paper argues that civilization demands a certain economy of pleasure, and that this economy is ensured by an apparatus constitutive of institutions of the law, both moral and juridico-political. The result is the increasing incorporation of life itself, in all its individuation and singularity, into the grasp of the law which suffocates life at its very source. Despite its apparent releasement of the libidinal sources of life in our modern world of utmost sophistication and technological advancement, the integrative violence of the law continues to operate under new guises, in a much more powerful

---

* Presented as lecture at Indira Gandhi National Open University, Delhi, on September 28, 2018.

manner which today is difficult for us to measure and understand.

I. Economy of Pleasure

Towards the end of his life Sigmund Freud comes to express his melancholy reflection about the prodigious price that humanity has to pay for its "civilization". It appears as if the foundation of civilization is constituted on a 'tragic denial': denial of the very elements of life, elements that constitute life *as* life, a denial to which Freud gives the unforgettable name "repression". The instituting drive of humanity, with its 'maximizing thrust' as Reiner Schürmann would call it, has paid a price too great for humanity to afford (Schürmann 2003). The edifice of civilization is built upon a 'tragic denial' of the elements that singularize us: the result is an edifice that conceals, behind the monumental features of its visible visage, its 'document of barbarism' to which Walter Benjamin invites us to reflect upon (Benjamin 1968: 253-64).

Already a few decades before Freud, Friedrich Nietzsche delineated for us a genealogy of this loss and the logic of this strange economy of civilization that he calls, in his own incomparable manner, "reversal". From Plato to Hegel, the history of metaphysics is understood as an ever more intense realization of this logic of reversal to which Nietzsche even assigns some "steps" or "stages": the Platonic reversal of elevating to the supreme significance the last evaporating reality, and downgrading of the most vital forms of life to the most degraded level (Nietzsche 1990). This reversal of "reality" which the very economy of self-preservation demands upon it, finds its most metaphysical expression in Hegel's metaphysics of Absolute Concept that banishes all that is sensuous, singular and riddle-some unconscious of life, and subjugates them, by a metaphysical violence, to the last evaporating reality called "Absolute Concept". The concept, the Hegelian concept of the concept, does not know pleasure. There is no *pleasure* of the concept. All that is tragic, "Dionysian", enigmatic "becoming" of life that is generous and magnanimous enough to squander itself, is set to put into "work" at the service of the last evaporating reality called the "concept".

This is the logic of the capital as Marx, a contemporary of Nietzsche saw it; it is the logic of production and investment, production of values constitutive of the whole modern economy called "capitalist". There can be "worklessness" only at the service of work, in sight of production, in sight of its possible return to profit, which is best exemplified in the economy of holidays. The secularization of the religious concept of "Sabbath" has transformed into "holidays" (which is deprived of all its holiness) which workers can have once a week so that on Monday they can be even more productive. This is the exact reversal of the religious logic of the Sabbath. God too rested on the seventh day, which is the holiest of days, for work here is performed in sight of rest, where receives it meaning from its Sabbath. Behind this idea of Sabbath is a peculiar idea of God as much as of the human: the human who enjoys Sabbath, like God, is not primarily *homo oikonomia.* In other words, the humanity of the human cannot be exhaustively determined as economic-labouring-producing being; rather, the plenitude of his being is realized precisely in Sabbath where life itself is consecrated and made holy. In contrast to it, the secularizing logic of modern civilization has come to determine the human as essentially *homo oikonomia.* Pleasure *qua* pleasure, pleasure in itself, is a waste, the excreta, a useless expenditure which the apparatus of civilization necessarily produces in order to re-incorporate it into the circular return of the same. Hence the necessity felt to superimpose upon the possibility of enjoying pleasure *qua* pleasure the attributes of the law that comes from institutions of morality as much as institutions of the juridico-political order: pleasure must be granted, provided that it serves the *oikonomia* of civilization, to its profit and preservation, for there is something in this pleasure *qua* pleasure that is radically workless and unprofitable, that refuses to return into the same, that is squandered away without being at the service of benefit. Pleasure *qua* pleasure, to put it simply, is useless, unproductive, and dangerous; to say with Georges Bataille, it is a "sovereign" element of our life.

The idea of civilization, specifically the civilization that we have call "modernity", is grounded upon this economic determination of the "human", and upon such an economization and regulation of sensation—of pleasure—in sight of profit: the profit of meaning and knowledge, not just the profit of wealth. Various institutions of our civilization provide such "schooling", with its operative principle of discipline and punish, with its rewards and constraints, whether it is the judicial institution or moral customs, schools or workplaces, factories or military institutions. They all carry the civilizing mission of economizing, minimizing and regularizing the pleasure of the individual so that only the pleasure that cannot be squandered away can be made available. With the most sophisticated methods supplied by institutions of knowledge—methods that classify and order phenomena with its law—they carry the civilizing mission of maximizing profit that incorporates individuals into masses, groups, categories, concepts, numbers and attributes. The 'tragic denial' of life through repression, sexual repression above all, is at once a process of de-individuation, and incorporation of individuals into bodies of norms that are prescripted and assigned in a pre-determinate manner that fixes individuals with the powerful gaze of the law. The law, whether it is juridical or moral, or even so-called "natural law", serves such an *oikonomia* of pleasure; it does this by *subjecting* us to those attributes or categories, anonymous and impersonal, of the law, thereby denying those pleasures and little deaths that singularize us, and make us un-incorporated beings without attributes and qualities.

II. Pleasure without Economy

Where is, then, the danger of pleasure lies—pleasure that is not constricted by the law, moral or juridical—pleasure that is not constrained into an attenuated variation of economy that constitutes the order of the world? It is the potential suspension of the law which pleasure threatens us with: it is here lies the true danger, but also the seduction, of pleasure; for what seduces us to pleasure is not the fulfilment of the law but its potential transgression, or even its momentary suspension; for what calls us to pleasure is its potential excess that cannot be pinned down to knowledge, to meaning, or to any tangible, enduring profit: plenitude that squanders itself away, and impoverishes itself in expenditure, and makes itself, once more, useless; pleasure that cannot be possessed and have, for, in a sense, no one can "have" pleasure. In other words, pleasure belongs neither to the order of "being" nor that of "having": this negativity of pleasure, that is, pleasure which cannot be assigned to any concept or knowledge by any order of discourse, is its very affirmation of becoming-excess-in-impoverishment, either below or above the law, each time it comes to the individual, to each one alone, separately, even when we are with the other or others. Even when it occurs within the prescripted institutions of the juridical-moral world-order, pleasure may still open us up to the "experience"—if one can still call it "experience"—of the non-inscripted and the un-prescripted, that which momentarily de-subjectivizes us, and in turn giving us to the solitude, individualizes us, in an individuation without "being" and "having". For pleasure, giving and receiving, is without possession, and hence, without the "values" that mark the economy of the world: it cannot be evaluated on the basis of any equivalences, pleasure that is without economy.

Pleasure threatens to suspend the law. An even more interesting proposition is: the law invents this danger for itself—that is, its own potential suspension—that pleasure is supposed to strike it with, for the law demands a principle supposedly antagonistic to itself in order to legitimatize itself by making the enjoyment of pleasure demonic and threatening to the order of civilization and culture. This exhibits, precisely hereby, the precarious foundation of our civilization: the order of civilization is constantly threatened, in an imagined or in a real manner, by little pleasures of the senses that individuals, alone or in groups, invent and enjoy, even those harmless ones, like masturbation alone. That pleasure can also be invented, and discovered for the first time, pleasure that is found where one never imagined before it existed there: this incessant potentiality of ever new invention of pleasure is always at odds with the operating principle of the law which tends to fix, once and for all if possible, "experiences" with categories and attributes, concepts and meanings. Multiplication, with its endless nuances and shades, nameless differences and imperceptible sensations, belong to the possibility of pleasure; the law, on the other hand, tends to unify sensations under categories, under 'hegemonic fantasm', with its 'maximizing thrust' (Schürmann 2003). Pleasure opens us to those singularities that always occur as 'undertow' beneath 'the maximizing thrust' of categories, like the ubiquitous light of the day hides our mortality. Pleasure wounds us like a piercing event, always incalculable, appearing while disappearing, arriving while vanishing, opening us to its sudden eruption and to the momentary disruption of our subjectivity. A momentary transgression where lies the very stake of not-being-able to be the human subject the law assigns us to which we normally and normatively adhere within the measures of institutional economy.

At stake here, then, is the very question of the essence of humanity. The concept of civilization demands, concomitantly, a certain determination of humanity that is not just different, but qualitatively opposed to animality: the enjoyment of pleasure *as* pleasure is considered to be "brutish" and "animalistic". This opposition between "humanity" and "animality" is very constitutive of what we call "civilization". That is why someone like Hegel, inspired by Aristotle, determines the essence of humanity negatively: the birth of the human is the death of the animal. This birth of the human—for Aristotle this is the very moment of the birth of the political—is contemporary with the birth of language: the scream dies and speech takes its birth. The political being, bearing its right, is not the being who merely screams or howls, but speaks; she is not merely an animal who merely derives pleasure from the titillating touching of the skin but the one for whom this touching-smelling-and its pleasure and pain is only a moment within the normative order of the civilization. The whole possibility or impossibility of pleasure, sexual pleasure above all, is founded and constricted by the very definition of the essence of humanity upon which civilization erects its foundation. We are not supposed to experience a certain mode of sexual pleasure which does not conform to the very "essence" or "nature" of humanity, the human who is antagonistic to or even a negation of "the animal".

Correlate to this Aristotelian linguistic distinction between scream and speech is the distinction between pleasure/pain and just/unjust: *the zoo politikon*, the political being, is one who primarily makes the distinction between just and unjust. In other words, speech is the very possibility of making the distinction between just and unjust, and such a being alone, who speaks and not merely screams, is the political being (Aristotle 1932: 11). Here the very possibility of the political is derived from the opposition between the human (who has *logos*) and the animal (who merely has a voice): the essence of humanity, whose humanity lies in being *political*, is not the being of pleasure and pain, but s/he who, negating the claims of pleasure and pain, can elevate itself to make the distinction between just and unjust. Here pleasure that cries and moans is tacitly determined as "animalistic": it falls below *logos* from which alone the possibility of the political can be derived.

Why, then, pleasure *as* pleasure is objection of suspicion? For sexual pleasure reaches the very limit of "humanity" as the limit of possibility, as it were, and poses as negativity, even though in a momentary manner, that suspends the order of the law. Making the calm distinction between the cry and speech indeterminate in the most imperceptible and incalculable manner possible, pleasure delivers the human to that zone of non-distinction from where the human does not completely emerge unscathed and untouched from animality. This negativity is not, unlike the negativity of the concept as Hegel propounds, a work, but a cunning negativity which puts work into its service so as to undo it. This worklessness, as Maurice Blanchot calls it, unworks in advance the whole logic of *oikonomia* of the *homo,* and produces an extra, or an excess, in its very impoverishment, that does not yield to profit once more. An expenditure, an unproductive-fruitless expenditure that makes the human of pure *oikonomia* other than a mere economic being: the human dispossessed of its economy and of its possession (of its "essence"). In other words, at stake is the very logic of the human being: heterogeneous to this economy of being of the law, Nietzsche's genealogy exposes us openly to the heteronomy of life, life *as* life, life heteronymous to *nomos;* it is that suspension of the *nomos*, of the law that metaphysics establishes in its 'the maximizing thrust' of language through strange reversals (through which the last evaporating reality becomes the supreme reality which the concept grasps).

III. Sade My Neighbour

Such suspension of the law occurs in the unbearable, unreadable and disgusting writings of Marquis de Sade. What Sade's incomparable writing exhibits is something that normative logic of pleasure represses. Generally we make the distinction—the distinction that constitutes the very norm of pleasure—of pleasure and pain into an oppositional and incommensurable one: pleasure as the avoidance of pain, and pain as the absence of pleasure. Sade's writing makes this static distinction (which is constitutive of the economy of pleasure), if not disappear, but at least an indeterminate one: pleasure and pain, in their dynamic *becoming*-pleasure and *becoming* pain, or, in their dynamic pleasure-*becoming*-pain and pain-*becoming*-pleasure, dissolves pleasure or pain as "states" or "categories". As if pain lies as an undertow, as potentiality, in each experience of pleasure, and offers, from its dark underground, to the very possibility of experiencing it; as a result, pleasure refuses to be "atomized" and categorized in the purity of a state. That there can be pleasure even in pain, which amounts to "cruelty" by the economic logic of any moral law, even juridical one: this cruelty is subversion of the economic law of pleasure itself. It is not simply the "aesthetic" pleasure, pleasure which is aesthetized (and anaesthetized) and made beautiful by the economic operation of the law: it is rather pleasure against pleasure, pleasure that touches the unbearable and repulsive, pleasure that displaces, in some indeterminate manner, the very human subject who knows pleasure *as* pleasure, and pain *as* pain.

This Sade achieves by writing itself, in writing creative works of imagination and fiction, in a language that revolts all sense of decorum and sobriety. What is revolting about Sade is not so much about these abominable practices of sexuality but writing, writing itself, this language of imagination itself, this whole thing called Sade-literature; what is revolting is not that Sade himself may have practised it—for Sade himself may have been least sadistic—but that he wrote it at all, and wrote it down in the most sordid manner possible. It is this literary quality of language that has the immense and prodigious power of evoking disgust, and yet, this is precisely Sade's intention: to disgust, to produce the most unattractive writing possible, to repulse our most cherished moral feelings of decorum and sensitivity. Sade wrote so as not to be read. Who writes not to be read? To attract morality to himself, he must write the most unreadable writing. Sade did not kill anyone, unlike the revolutionaries of the French Revolution: all that he did, for 32 years of prison life, is just writing, literature whose power lies in its very powerlessness, so much so that one can be imprisoned just for putting down something on paper. This is the enigma of Sade's writing: literature, literature of mere words which does not kill any more, which is supposed to be the most powerless activity of a man, has a tremendous power that fascinates us for ages, has a power to revolt the immense edifice of our morality that civilization has constituted for ages. That nobody dares to justify Sade, even now, even by the most adamant apologists of Sade: this precisely is what is fascinating about him, this man of writing of sheer immorality and cruelty. Here writing itself seeks to transgress the law, whether it is the moral law or the juridico-political one. What Sade's exploits here is the explosive power of *reading* itself, not so much the practices of these abominable sexual pleasures: there is a pleasure of reading Sade which explodes all sense of moral economy and regulation, where reading is *sexualized* and *erotized*, where reading becomes equivalent to sexual pleasure with all its antinomic effects. It is the pleasure of reading and writing that is explosive: it is this pleasure, this sexuality of reading and writing, which needs to be confined and constrained by the moral law of civilization. In other words, what Sade does is to *sexualize* language, makes the human language into an experience of cruel pleasure or pleasurable cruelty. The human language of *logos* which is supposed to make the distinction between just and unjust appear in it, is pierced through by cries and moans of pleasure and pain, by the trembling of skin that voices out without being completely transformed into concepts, categories and attributes of the law.

Despite being abominable and disgusting, or, precisely because of this, Sade is seductive, for it gives us glimpses into that region of impossible possibility which the law itself, negatively though, hints at: that which transgresses the law. As if, the law should be there only to be transgressed; as if, by its rigorous institutions of the law, it indirectly and elliptically invites us to its very possible transgression. In other words, the law seduces us to pleasure precisely by forbidding or economizing it. If there were no law at place, would there have been transgression? As if, transgression of the law and the institution of the law have the co-birth; or even, if one pushes this understanding a bit far, one may even say that transgression has *always already* begun, not temporally though, at the very moment of institution of the law. Transgression is the logical presupposition of the institution of the law.

The law itself, at the very instance of its positing, needs something that potentially transgresses it, which it needs to restrain and economize, something that exceeds it and impoverishes it in turn. That means, the economy of the law itself demands the non-economy of pleasure to the point of cruelty, not as consequence of the law but as a the very structural opening of itself to its institution and constitution.

Hegel has a penetrating gaze into this instituting character of the law. In the famous section on the moral order of his *Phenomenology of Spirit,* Hegel observes how even the unconscious transgression of the law calls forth the retributive strike of punishment. Here lies the integrative violence of the law: the law designates the one whom it incorporates within its fold as already a transgressor and a criminal, at least potentially, it does not matter whether she will ever transgress the law or not. Here is the cunning of the law through which particular citizens are subsumed with 'the maximizing thrust' of its language.

Such integrative violence of the law considers pleasure as already a potential transgression of the law, unless pleasure is enjoyed within the bounds of the legitimate institutions of the moral order, such as marriage and family; in other words, the licit and legitimate pleasure is the incorporated pleasure, pleasure incorporated within the means and end structure of the law. To ensure this, the moral law seeks the support of the juridical law, constituting thereby an ideological state apparatus that assigns pleasure that has its end in itself, and that refuses to be a means to an end external to itself as something transgressive, condemnable and illicit.

IV. Free Love

It is precisely against this integrative violence of the law that the movement of "free love" of the early 20th century came into being: the free love here is precisely that love which is to be freed *from* the coercive force of the law. Here love is not understood as mere hedonistic-libertine freedom to have sexual pleasure with anyone that one likes, but the freedom of the individuals to be with one-another in a relationship of love and of pleasure, out of their own consent, which must be freed from the law and from the legitimized institution of marriage. The notion of free love is to be freed, not only from the law but from the restricted understanding of love itself which constrains love to a monogamous and mono-amorous relationship. It recognizes, and puts into question the normative concept of love which, even when it is practised outside or before marriage, or even without marriage, always takes its paradigmatic meaning from the institution of marriage: erotic love is always considered to be possible only between two individuals, as marriage is by definition monogamous.

It is not for nothing that in a country like India, which never has experienced any movement like "free love", an extra-marital affair on the part of a man (not a woman) with a married woman, without the consent of the other man, is still considered to be a criminal offence in the 21st century. It not only presupposes that a married woman is the private property of her husband, it also considers the economy of pleasure within marriage—and marriage by definition is heterosexual, monogamous and mono-amorous—to be the inviolate, sanctified and consecrated paradigm of all erotic relationships possible between humans, more constrictively, between a man and a woman.

V. Love with Benefits

Now at the beginning of this new millennium, flowers of love and pleasure seem to be blooming in a more glorious light than ever before. Every object of production and consumption today, right from mango juices to a pair of shoes, from perfume to soaps, is sexualized or erotized in the advertisements, promising an abundance of limitless pleasure. With the plethora of online dating rising sky-high, and emergence of varied sorts of relations, like "friends with benefits" and "no strings attached", and "live-in", etc, it may appear that sexuality and love are now finally liberated and emancipated completely from the prison-house of morality and the law.

A slightly deeper look, however, gives us a different understanding of these phenomena. In today's 'society of the spectacle'—as Guy Debord uses this term (Debord 1995)—nothing is more spectacular or more profitable than pleasure in the global marketplace of mass-consumption. Everything, even the least sexual thing or the most asexual thing, must be sexualized to be profitable: in this universalization of so-called sexualization that touches every aspect of our life today, a life that feeds itself upon the virtual world of fantastic enjoyment, nothing seems to be more missing than truly a form of life freed from the grasp of the law. One fitting example today is that of online dating in the world which is so powerfully controlled by all powerful social media. The sky-high rising of online dating has become a source of such profit for these owners that millions of lonely individuals in the lonely metropolitan cities of an overwhelming crowd are now reduced to mere "customers" for these multinational companies. The immense loneliness of lonely individuals in crowded cities, looking for love and enjoyment, for friendship and companionship, has now become the target of immense profit-making multinational businesses. What now takes place is meeting with other individuals, who are equally lonely though, and yet without truly encountering them, for the other(s) do not appear to us any more as someone to be encountered in her absolutely singular individual being, but as someone with whose encounter some pleasure, like profit, can be elicited. Love and pleasure are once more incorporated, in a much more overwhelming manner, and in a much more powerful apparatus of totalization, in a system to which we individuals willy-nilly participate, without anyone asking us to. Nobody forces us to join online dating sites or in social media like Facebook and Instagram, and yet, all of us are forced, by an invisible, anonymous and impersonal force—which is a force without force—to participate in today's system of totalization. This force without force, which is precisely thus the force in its nakedness, never ceases to measurelessly incorporate us into the new world-order of economy for which pleasure and love are nothing other than pure fantasy, an elusive and unattainable object of desire: we now daily live a life incorporated much more powerfully within the means-end structure of the economic law. It is an overwhelming paradox that today's world, which takes care so much in socialization through social media and online dating sites, etc., individuals are lonelier than ever before, and nothing is today more difficult than truly to encounter another human individual in her absolute singularity. This is the new barbarism of today's extremely sophisticated and technologically advanced civilization.

This paradox is only symptomatic of the immense prices that we are paying for our civilization: on the one hand, the online dating and "friends with benefits" are becoming "in" in today's world of erotic mass-consumption; on the other hand, a new puritanism of morality is emerging at the time, economizing our need for love, companionship and pleasure—in the words, our whole erotic being-with and being-together—by various ways censoring our erotic-amorous life in the name of the heterosexual, monogamous and mono-amorous institution of marriage which is for us, still now, the only consecrated and inviolable paradigm of our eroticism. Here and now, as before, marriage is still considered, on economic terms, as the inviolable sexual contract between two heterosexual humans: the need of love, of friendship and companionship are still reduced to an economy of sexual contract within marriage, a contract which is assured by the anonymous force of the law. More or more love and pleasure seek to fulfil our life itself as freed from the prison of the law, more is the law capturing our life in ever new guises, abandoning love and pleasure to an unattainable goal.

BIBLIOGRAPHY

Aristotle, *Politics*, trans. H. Rackham (Cambridge: Harvard University Press, 1932).

Benjamin, Walter, 'Theses on the Philosophy of History' in *Illuminations*, trans. Harry Zohn with an Introduction by Hannah Arendt (New York: Schocken Books, 1968), 253-264.

Debord, Guy, *The Society of the Spectacle*, trans. Donald Nicholson-Smith (MIT Press, 1995).

Freud, Sigmund, *Civilization and Its Discontents*, ed. James Strachey (W.W. Norton & Company, 2010/1929).

Nietzsche, Friedrich, *The Twilight of the Idols and The Anti-Christ: Or How to Philosophize with a Hammer*, trans. R.J. Hollingdale (Penguin Classics, 1990).

Schürmann, Reiner, *Broken Hegemonies*, trans. Reginald Lily (Indiana University Press, 2003).

The Exodus of Writing*

I. The Outside

The subject of discussion here is "text, context and interpretation". However, I will begin speaking mainly of "writing", and only then that of "text" (but not "Book", and we will see why), "context", that is to say: co-texts, and "interpretation", that is to say: to expound the law of the text, or the meaning of the text. But what does it mean to say "meaning" of the text; or, better, what is the *meaning* of meaning? Similarly, we are immediately confronted with the question: what is the law of the law? To complicate the question even more, and in a way that touches the heart of the problematic that interests me today: what is the meaning of the law that constitutes or

* Plenary speech in the seminar on *Text, Context and Interpretation*, Department of English, Gauhati University, January 23-24, 2018.

deconstitutes a text? What is it that intimates the relation, at once enigmatic and difficult, between "meaning" and "the law" (not that of a particular, specific law, but that of the law *as such*)? The question of the text—which we will see that it always already implies writing, or, literature—immediately and ineluctably poses itself this question: is there a law in and of literature? Is the language of literature or writing—writing not opposed to speech, but outside of the opposition—exhausted in the language of the law? Or rather, at stake here is precisely the inexhaustion of writing which, in its refusal—and this is the word we can borrow from Maurice Blanchot—in its refusal to be pinned down by the concept or by meaning, opens up a plenitude that at once marks the destitution of literature, destitution which in turn cannot be incorporated, transfixed and grasped by the force of the law. If this were so (this inexhaustion of writing), writing or literature somehow exceeds the logic of the law while passing through it, traversing it, contaminating it, and even interrupting it: writing that opens up the text and makes the text an un-enclosed space, cannot be said, strictly speaking, to be the language of the law and of the law of meaning. What, then, the interpreter interprets when s/he interprets a text?: she expounds, that is, she makes the text "ex"-pound, that is to say, to transcend—as in "ex-tasy" or "ex-sistence"—to open to the outside of the book, outside the Book. What opens the Book, and well-comes (and welcomes) the text—in the *coming-well*, in the *jouissance*, in the *l'avenir*—is writing.

What comes, in this *coming*, in this *coming-well*, in the *jouissance* of the text, is writing itself, writing *to come*, in the sense of *l' avenir*—to come. From the work of Jacques Derrida, we have learnt to differentiate, in the *spacing* of this *differance*, between the tense future—*futur*—which is one tense among other tenses, and then, the *jouissance* of the "to come", *l'avenir*! The *jouissance* of writing does not become, unlike the tense *futur*, another presence in turn, for it has never become a presence, for it *always already* exceeds the immanence of all self-presence: such is writing *to come*, each *hic et nunc*, never belonging to any metaphysics of presence.

What, then, here at stake is the thought of the outside: the exodus of writing, in all its rigour and severity, the "ex" of the exodus. Writing to come, which *always and already* is *to come*—and this is what we call as the event future anterior –is also, at the very same instance, without belonging to any *sync* of synchrony (*sync-chronos*), a going-out, the ex- of exodus, an infinite departure, the Odysseus who never returns home but is always *ex-posed* on the tempestuous sea of peril and danger. To be *ex-posed*, to be posed *ex-*: this is the Odysseus of the desert, not the Odysseus who comes back, and is always coming back, to his Penelope, but he who, having come, already *de-parts* to the unknown. In French language, to interpret is to do *exposition* of the text under consideration, that is to say: to posit outside, to ex-posit, to posit ex-, and hence, to non-posit. *To come* to the text, in order to exposit it, is to posit it ex- and to expose it: to make the text de-part, to render it a-part, like a pair of torn shocks which makes (as Hegel said once) consciousness appear, apart from all closures, from all enclosures, to open the text, once more, which means, infinitely. To read a text, to interpret a text, is to make the ship of the text sail on the exodus of infinite writing to come, to the expose the text and to expose oneself, to the exodus, each time anew and each time differently. In each reading, if it is genuine and attentive reading, the text is born anew, and it is a new text: the text is like Lazarus who comes alive from death, for, as St. Paul reminds us, "the letter killeth, but the spirit giveth life" (2 Corinthians 3:6). The law is the work of death, but writing—and also reading—is not life opposed to death; it is life after death: it is sur-vive, a survival, the survival of the text through and beyond the reader, survival to the extent that the text is opened up once more, from all closures and enclosures of self-presence of meaning and the law, to its life *to come*. To interpret a text, in the sense of ex-position, is to posit it ex—(outside); it also has the sense of opening the text outside all "positions" and all "op-positions", and hence, outside the dialectical law of *Aufhebung*.

This is to say: the space of writing, or "the space of literature" as Maurice Blanchot calls, is exodus: the space of the outside, not the "outside" dialectically opposed to "inside", not that opposition that will have Hegelian *Aufhabung*, but outside of all presence and absence, of being and its dialectical counterpart non-being. The condition of writing, or, of literature is the non-condition, or un-condition of exodus: to ex-sist outside home, without dwelling, without the auto-poesis of any autochthony, without bearing any aboriginal origin: the exodus of writing! Writing is Odysseus, not with Penelope, but on the high sea of tempest. The desert or the sea, in all its incalculable and demonic weather, with all risks of peril and of non-return: this exodus knows no *oikonomia*—the economy—of meaning or of the law. The exodus is the non-economic event par excellence. This exodus of writing or of literature makes writing in-exhaustible to the institutional determination of it; like an infinite sur-plus, the enigma of writing infinitely destitutes the institute and the institutional foundation of the community, and exceeds all economy of return. Maurice Blanchot calls such a literary community an "unavowable community", and Jean Luc Nancy calls it "the inoperative community": the coming community, the community *to come.*

II. The End of the Book

It is the exodus of writing that I will speak on today, exodus that has always already parted my lips when I am about to utter the word, and the movement of my hand on this empty, blank paper. At the inception, of writing, there is the parting and departing: between the pair of lips that opens the void; between my hand and this empty, blank paper. It is only on this condition—which is also the very non-condition—of this exodus, can there come to exist something like "text", "context" and "interpretation"; or, better to say, what we call "text", "context" and "interpretation" are *always and already* writing, and are in exodus, outside the Book but passing through the Book, traversing the Book so as to go outside the Book: the ruse of writing! The Book constricts the exodus movement of interminable writing, and assigns it, by the force of the law, the designation and the destination of meaning. For this is the meaning of all meaning and destination: that, it is the *means*, already inscribed in the structural logic of "means and end", or, "means to an end". Is it not the very logic of the law? The language of the law is the language of meaning: law uses a means to an end! This is its *raison d'art*, its legitimate use, or, if you allow me to say: this is its legitimate violence.

We have mentioned above: to interpret has the sense of ex-position. To posit—the German verb word *setzen*—is the very root of *Gesetz*, of the law. Walter Benjamin in his essay *Critique of Violence* draws out hereby the very metaphysical foundation of the law: the positing character of the law, which is what Benjamin calls "the law-positing violence". The metaphysical foundation of the law is its positing-character, its thetic-character, and its violence is the *arché-violence* of the law. Benjamin names this arché-violence as "the mythic violence", which is, the law-positing violence and the violence that results from its preserving.

Benjamin then goes on to distinguish another violence from this mythic violence: this other violence, which is other than violence, other than all positing and preserving violence, and hence, other than the violence that results from the mythic foundation of the law, is called "the divine violence". Benjamin associates this divine violence with the messianic conception of redemption and with expiation without spilling blood. This messianic expiation is to be distinguished from the tragic-dialectic atonement of the Hegelian *Aufhebung*. The messianic suspension of the law is the *ex-positio* or *ex-positing* of all thetic act of the concept. If positing is the violent origin of the law, then ex-position, or interpretation, or ex-pounding, is that which opens the text to outside the law. *The one who interprets a text reads it in the light of redemption.* The messianic light of redemption redeems us from the violence of all thetic-positing of the law. A work of art from which beauty emanates, a work of philosophy from where emanates the serene glow of truth, and even from the work of translation that participates in the pure language of naming, and, if you want to add, in our interpretation and exposition of a text, there occurs our participation in the coming messianic redemption. To interpret a text does not mean to find out the definite, final and ultimate meaning of the text lying at its furthest recesses; it is rather to participate in the messianic language of sober prose that releases so many messianic possibilities immanent in the text and are enclosed in it. Exposition ex-posits these possibilities, releases and opens up its explosive possibilities that burst out of the closure of the Book, out of the enclosure of the system or of totality. In that sense, interpretation is always already infinite in its possibility, though finite in each mode of its occurrence: it is the infinitude outside the totality of meaning, outside the system of relation, outside the totality of knowledge. The infinite interpretation, or infinite exposition, is also an infinite contestation—of closures, totalities, systems that work by the force of the law, by the violence of the concept, by the transfixing gaze of meaning.

So many things, then, are at stake: the Book and the text, context and co-texts, interpretation but also inter-penetration, and above all, writing—this exodus of writing—and the law, the meaning of the law, the force of the law, its penetrating gaze and its violence. The violence of the law constricts the interminable and incessant movement of writing without destination, and assigns it a "destination", fixes its end—its "telos" –and thus, thereby, assigning it the "origin", the *arché*: the archaeology of the Book has also its teleology, which is to say, the arché-teleology constitutes the Book as such, the Book par excellence, the Book of all books. The arché-teleology is the innermost ground of unity of the Book where *arché* (the beginning) and the *telos* (the end) coincide: the result is the geometrical figure of the circle, eternally returning to the same, like the time of the capital, like the economy of presence, whose auto-poesis is called "myth". The language of the Book is mythic auto-poesis, for what myth itself is if not the "auto-poesis" par excellence?

III. The Text

The text is, then, to be seen as something other than, and otherwise than the Book. Hegel calls his Book "System" that he presents in his *Encyclopedia*: the totality of relations grounded on the principle—the *arché*—immanent to the system itself; there is nothing outside, no ex-, and no trans-, of the Book if not it is the Book's very, and its own outside: outside that is thought on the basis of the inside, for it is the outside *of* the inside. If one takes into account Maurice Blanchot's "thought of the outside" here—as Michel Foucault does by naming this thought of the outside as the thought of the non-positive affirmation—then the thought of the outside that Blanchot takes pain to think is not the outside that belongs to the Book as its very dialectical assertion (which is not alien to negation but makes negation is its very axis). Blanchot calls this thought of the outside "the absence of the Book", not the absence that is dialectically opposed to the Book but the absence that, traversing through the Book, exposes the immanence of self-presence to the unthinkable difference. Interpretation, or exposition, here, uncovers another sense: to expose something to something, to the incalculable and unknowable, to the surprise of the event, to the surprise of the coming, *l' avenir*: the dialectical movement of knowledge suddenly comes to a standstill. This affirmation of the outside, which Plato knew and called it "wonder" or "astonishment"—the very origin of philosophy—is the affirmation without position and positing: it is rather ex-positing or de-positing of knowledge; an affirmation which is neither assertion nor negation, but outside...the infinite, interminable, exodus of writing. What is exposed in our exposition of the text is not the potency of meaning, the power and force of the concept, but the destitution or fragility of writing that, without positing another force against the force of the law, traverses through the text, and makes its cry resound, as the French word *écriture* shows: the *cri-* the cry—of *écriture*. The New Testament Gospels speak of the cry of the one in the wilderness, the one from the desert, the one who suffers the exodus of existence, namely, John the Baptist. The one who, being abandoned, cries in the desert, cries for what is "to come": such is the exposition of the text, the text of the world, un-enclosed by the "beyond" which the world knows not. The world is torn apart from its foundation with the arrival, with the coming—of the Other; the truth of the world—the text of the world, the textile of the world, the fabric of the world—is undone when the Other, the Messiah comes: the Book can, then, never return into the same; the circle cannot, again, be closed; the mythic foundation of the world is interrupted, once again.

IV. The Cry

Not surprisingly, the myth of the eternal return of the same is the myth par excellence: exodus, according to this myth, is mere privatum, a provisional but necessary diremption that always brings the same Odysseus back home once again. The myth, in all its pathos of origin and end, of its *arché-telos*, then serves, in all communities, as their founding principle, as the grounding *arché*, as the hegemonic principle that elicits legitimacy from us, whether it is the *arcanum* of the racist Aryan identity, in all its fury of "blood and soil", or it is the myth of the paradisal communist society that Stalin effectively used, or misused. Every hegemonic regime effectively uses or misuses, and appeals to, such mythic foundation that, auto-poetically, solidifies its claim to an autochthonous origin, as if there is something like a pure, uncontaminated, Aryan race whose purity is assured through the purity of blood and soil. The metaphysical violence of this act of mythic foundation is not only demonstrated by Walter Benjamin in his essay *The Critique of Violence*, but also by Ernst Cassirer in his important work *The Myth of the State*.

In his much discussed book *The Inoperative Community* Jean Luc Nancy shows how writing or literature infinitely interrupts, and renders inoperative the mythic foundation of a community that tends to close itself up, like the circle that always returns to the same, like the economy of the capital. The exodus of writing—the ex- of exodus—never returning to the same, interrupts the immanence of self-presence that every myth claims: what, then, we see here is the text, and not the Book, the exodus of the text, exposed open to the *futurity to come* which, as I said before, is not the tense *futur* but the *l'avenir*: *l'avenir* that is not which comes in order to pass by, but that which is always *to come*. The text, existing—ex-sisting, this being-outside—here and now, *hic et nunc*, is still, is *always already*, *to come*: this is the eternal *jouissance* of the text, an impossible idea, the very idea of the impossible, but affirmative nevertheless, without any thetic positing and negating.

The text that we see here, this one, is still *coming*. It is still *to come*. It is still *to come* having come. Having come, it is surviving in my hand, under my gaze, with my parted lips. It of course bears the history of many shipwrecks, but this is the unfinished history; its history is interminable and incessant: "this insane game of writing", as Mallarmé remarked once! Context, or co-text, is the inoperative community of these incomplete histories, full of many explosive messianic possibilities. The interpreter does not so much penetrate the text with the violence of his or her gaze, unless one is always already penetrated by the text so much that all interpretation becomes inter-penetration; the interpreter rather makes apparent these messianic possibilities that are immanent in the text but are enclosed, or encrypted, existing like ciphers or crypt. The interpreter de-crypts, or de-ciphers, these nameless messianic possibilities, and renders the text open once again in the glow that emanates from the star of redemption.

The exodus of writing: the infinite and interminable refusal to be bound by the logic of *oikonomia;* infinite interruption of any mythic return to the same; this movement whose secret password is a promise: not any promise but the very promise of *to-come*, the promise of promises itself, the very promise of redemption. The interpreter reads the text, along with other texts as co-texts, not by the force of the law that reduces literature or writing as a mere institution, as a classifiable entity in the order of discourses within the universe of knowledge; he or she reads texts in the light of redemption that infinitely exceeds the institutional moment of any discourse, and transcends the positing act of codification and systematization. To begin interpreting a text, then, is to begin another text, once again, another exodus, and another "insane game of writing".

"The insane game of writing": the "cri"– the cry—of *écriture* is the cry of the desert, of the exodus, whose secret password is promise, the promise of the community *to come*. This literary community, unavowable and inoperative, is not the community sharing a common—the *Koinon*—essence where every entity gets fused into a mythic identity. The word "fascio", from which has come "fascism", means such mythic auto-saying; it evokes, provokes and invokes a community grounded upon the mythic auto-poesis of fusion: this is the mythic violence of all dwelling and habitation to which the work of Emmanuel Lévinas draws our attention at the wake of destruction of six million Jews and two world wars. Irreducible to the cognitive violence of the concept, the strange trembling—this *cri* of *écriture*—of literature evokes a community, not based upon "the blood and soil", but the community of the exodus, which is the context of all possible texts, the messianic community. It is in this community that each interpretation, singular each time, is carried out where each interpretation, once more, opens the text, beyond all closures of dwelling and habitation. Such is the exodus of writing.

Who is the Dalit?*

It is imperative now to think the political at a different level than has ever been before, to think the political beyond strategies, negotiations and playing cards (caste card, gender card, minority card, etc.). This means that to demand justice in the name of a repressed caste or a gender in itself is not reducible to playing cards, or doing politics at the level of strategies. This is precisely what is difficult to understand today: if the very idea of 'politics' is overdetermined or exhausted in the strategic moves that we play in the realm of practical affairs to secure specific rights or conditioned profits, and thereby mobilizing forces against forces, whether in the name of a specific caste or gender, then I am not primarily doing politics. What I can be said to be doing then, and also thinking and professing then, is something else and at another level, in another

---

* Earlier published in *Indian Cultural Forum*.

manner and in another tongue.

Therefore, what I am and the position I assume today, cannot be understood by the plethora of attributes that are thrown at me, whether well-wishing me or accusing me of playing cards (caste politics, minority politics or whatever): they don't understand what I am trying to do here. I am not a 'communist' or 'dalit' understood as an attribute or predicate which I will strategically use to gain specific rights through negotiations with the ones in power: Dalit is rather the name through which the immense and immeasurable waves of millennium long injustice and savageries have passed and are continuously passing through, and that are clamouring for an infinite, unconditional and non-negotiable justice in the name of which specific rights are to be secured in the domain of the political. This fine distinction between 'dalit' as an attribute and Dalit as 'the weak messianic power' as in Walter Benjamin: this irreducible difference is completely erased when people discuss my thought and my actions and my political practices. I indeed introduce, in writing and in my action in the political domain, a 'philosophy' of the political which consists of thinking that which infinitely exceeds, while passing through, the strategic politics of conditioned negotiations. This philosophy of the political is not a storehouse of maxims or theorems which one will strategically put into practice by filling up their empty forms: it can't, thus, be understood in the idiomatic gesture of regulative actions, as that happens in

Immanuel Kant's understanding of moral actions. It rather consists of introducing into the political the messianic intensity that does not exhaust itself in the conditioned realization of specific rights.

If one speaks of 'proletariat' now or of 'Dalit'—and it is necessary do so—it is only so that the proletariat destroys all other classes and while destroying them, itself too must pass away; so, it is with the 'Dalit': the absence of the Dalit in just society is precisely the consummate messianic instance in the name of which all political struggles, bearing the name 'Dalit', must be carried out. Therefore, the name 'Dalit' can be used today and must be used, only as the name of the unnameable. It is not a simple name: it evokes what remains and will remain unnameable until the infinite justice arrives. Like a dying man who wants life, the oppressed ones thus clamour for justice. Our existence, in its very finitude, does not want to be exhausted in mere negotiations for conditioned-practical rights. Only infinity saturates and consummates our existence. This is why justice is the infinite idea par excellence.

Therefore one must speak out today which means, precisely, to risk one's own existence, and yet, this risk is also the very movement that goes beyond by traversing the realm of death. S/he who does not speak knows no hope, for hope is the venturing beyond into the unknown. We must, then, clearly distinguish between the officially recognized "promotion" in the hierarchy of the academic institution and the true intellectual worth of a body of works that someone leaves behind. Only those who are working at the same intellectual and existential level as the scholar in question can really evaluate and appreciate the true worth of that form of life and that work. In the later sense, which is the true sense, I am "professor" already: While this first one—that is, "professor" in the hierarchy of the academic institution—is dubious at best, unless accompanied by the later, for it is often mere reduplication of social hierarchy into the academic situation, and it can be—as we all have eyes to see, unless one chooses to keep her eyes closed—manipulated and abused: by the technology of sheer quantification, by the political ideology that governs social relations, by the millennium-long social injustice and prejudice. It is this prejudice and injustice that is the stake and that is the question. Here and now.

The Precarious Democracy*

That "one of the biggest democracies of the world", as we fondly say, is so utterly precarious and fragile is now visible more than ever before. Behind the endless advertisements on which the regime spends so much tax payers' money, behind the spectacles that the regime is anxious to perform daily—that India is shining on the stage of the world-historical—the horror of the truth is too dazzling to be hidden: the truth of every civilization (as the philosopher Walter Benjamin reminds us with an insistence that we cannot ignore) is that it contains a document of barbarism. Any amount of empirical evidences, inexhaustible as they are, is always insufficient; we have to reach the fundamental ground which is nothing other than an irreparable fissure or a wound that has fundamentally torn apart the fabric of what we have learnt to call "democracy": a "cracy" or

* Earlier published in *Indian Cultural Forum.*

"regime" where the "demos" is essentially absent, and is held in abeyance, where it is always already withdrawn, not directly but by a cunning of reason which constitutes the administrative-bureaucratic rationality, or irrationality. This rationality works by reducing "demos" or "people" into quantifiable, classifiable and numerable entities that constitute the order of administration. Thus is produced the myth of reason, the myth of the political reason that serves as obedient servant to the regime at place.

Myth in this sense, then, is not opposed to reason; there is something like the myth of reason, as much as there is always a reason in every myth. Myth, far from having withdrawn from the horizon of our historical-political existence, constitutes the very foundation of political hegemonies. All political hegemonies legitimize themselves on mythic foundations and solicit normative obligations from us out of those mythic foundations. There is something like "the myth of the state", as the philosopher Ernst Cassirer calls it: the pure Aryan identity for the Nazi Socialists (Hitler), the idea of a messianic communist society that is forcibly enforced by human power (Mao, Stalin), and the idea of an aboriginal and autochthonous Hindu identity—just like the slogan of "blood and soil"—that is self-same, and which must be preserved in its purity by eliminating what it constitutes as its political enemy. All such myths of the state constitute their own political enemy who is to be extinguished, or to be kept subjugated by the violence of legitimate power.

The savage violence of legitimate power derives, legitimately—and this is the fissure and the wound—from the very reason of the state. This violence is the innermost possibility of the constituted order of democracy. This is why almost all fascist regimes of the past century have erupted from democracies that have legitimately exercised the savage violence.

It is this mythic foundation of the political hegemonic order of today's India—where extreme capitalism of mass consumption along with extremely advanced technology and the most regressive thinking, in cultural and social terms, belong together as a seamless whole—that explains the unspeakable, barbaric, tyrannical violence that we witness in India today. By using the mythic idea of Hindu-Aryan identity—which is, thus, the racist conception par excellence—the now hegemonic force (which has become hegemonic through a constitutionally legitimate manner, a possibility that is given in any constitutional-parliamentary democracy) claims to identify itself with the whole political order and social-historical existence: this is what Jacques Derrida calls "onto-theology of national humanism". A particular claims the position of the universal, and seeks complete totalization. What is absent here, in this democracy, is precisely the "demos": an undemocratic democracy that it has become, whose other name is fascism.

The racist Aryan-Hindu identity, mythical as it is, constitutes itself as opposed to its dialectical other: the

Dalit, the Muslims, the Christians, and women in some cases. This opposition is the very condition of possibility of the Aryan Hindu identity, and this identity, far from being primordial and aboriginal is precisely derived from these oppositions. Hence, this mythic identity is actually a historical and a historically derived identity through differences (where difference is understood as opposition). There does not exist, and has never existed pure identity of a Hindu race or a Hindu culture, or a Hindu civilization: it is the historical fabulization and transformation of this fable into a mythic identity which is then, a posteriori, derived from a mythic age and an ancient past.

Today, our democracy is Janus-faced: evoking and regressing to a millennium-long mythological past, and yet, buying the extremely advanced technology of this new millennium. The truth is that nobody, not even the most hard core Hindutva ideologue believes in this mythological past. This fable is evoked only to attain legitimate power of a hegemonic regime through democratic-constitutional means. The result is everywhere to be seen: Dalits are repressed, oppressed and slaughtered in the most barbaric manner possible, the Muslims are slaughtered for being Muslims, and women are now treated like slaves (even in a University like JNU and many other universities across the nation, administrations are now restricting women students in various manners and even planning to remove women studies departments from the universities). This unspeakable violence of the legitimate power is absolutely—ethically—illegitimate. The demonic violence of these evil forces arises out of the very reason of the hegemonic force: the necessity, for legitimacy, of political enemies which do not exist but must be produced, created, mythologized and naturalized. As if Hindus and Muslims are the natural enemies forever, which has never been so and which will never be so.

Towards an Understanding of the University[*]

Though at different historical periods dominant political hegemonies have sought to appropriate the University, recent years have witnessed this appropriation to an unsurpassed degree with a qualitatively greater intensity. It can only be compared to the 'nationalization' of the University-structure during the Nazi regime and during the historical epoch of Stalin. Here is the logic of what the French philosopher Jacques Derrida calls "onto-theology of national humanism": the false universal and universalization of a specific, particular claim (the claim of a particular people—let's say the Brahminical order of Hindu religion and culture to be the pan-Indian cultural phenomenon); the deification and mythologization of a collective fusion (this is the meaning of fascism: the

---

* Earlier published in *Indian Cultural Forum.*

word "fasces" means collective fusion) on an aboriginal consciousness (for example: "the blood and soil" ideology of the national socialists), whether that fusion is thought in terms of a radical purity (Aryan identity) or of a mythic continuum (marked by a "tradition" that identically persists through every moment of historical transformation).

With the withering away of the "social welfare" model of the nation state in the wake of the extreme form of neoliberal economic theology, the state is no longer an agent of social welfare but has become an industry among industries, or in fact, it has become the industry par excellence. In such a situation, when the Indian state has given up the "social welfare" model, and yet, on the other hand, has taken up the violent language of an extremely regressive and conservative form of nationalism, the University will be allowed only one *telos* (the goal and the purpose): the University must assimilate itself into the overwhelming structure of the neoliberal economy whose false universalization does not have to be opposed to the nationalism which is culturally based on the most obscure and the most primitive cultural confusion. The state can participate, as an industry or a corporate group, in the false universality of the newliberal economic machine that is fuelled by extremely advanced technological and bureaucratic tools, and at the same time, at the social and cultural level, it can remain as primitive and regressive as in the 5th century BC. This is how the nation-state can claim to appropriate the University which, by definition, exceeds all the logic of territory: the University, by definition, has to be universal. It is *the* universal *institution* par excellence because it destitutes—and is this *destitution* par excellence—of all economic logic of national closures.

Now this paradox is totally hinged by the aforesaid onto-theology: the universality of the University, by its very axiomatic being, is irreducible to the onto-theology of any and all national humanism. The paradox is that the University, residing within the geographical territory of a nation and even with the economic support of the government, exceeds all possible national closures in all futures to come. This is the scandal which no nationalism can hope to bear: the more extreme and brutal the form of nationalism becomes, the more intolerable becomes the *topos* (site or place) of the University for the order of the state. Thus, either the University has to be annihilated directly, which is impractical, or the place of the University is to be transformed and converted into the very productive and fecund source where the onto-theology of national humanism grows like "mushrooms after the rain" (Søren Kierkegaard).

Therefore, it is not surprising that in a premier University like the Jawaharlal Nehru University, the honourable Vice-Chancellor wants to reduce, in a typically technocratic-bureaucratic fashion, the whole University into a factory or industry. This is the typical gesture of an engineer, almost here in the social mode: a social engineering, if you like to say so. Behind this, and behind so many of his gestures, what is operating is the economic logic of technological rationality combined with the mystification of a primitive, mythic conservatism, the Brahminical order of engineering in the guise of an extreme, technologically sophisticated, economic and political domination.

It is not for nothing that Martin Heidegger could say that technology cannot think. The brutal assault on the Universities today has the purpose of creating a thoughtless order, the order that thoughtlessly—that is, without critiques, deconstructions, subversions, etc.—accepts the political and economic domination of the neoliberal Brahminism.

In Indian society, generally, we always have the weakness for engineering and the civil services. From very early on, we are ourselves engineered to be engineers and civil servants, and we think engineers and civil servants are the highest human beings ever. This is so pronounced that the dominant political parties, just before elections, suddenly build bridges and repair roads (in other words, do a bit of engineering), and the mass of people are overwhelmed by the illusion of the social progress that is made in two months' time! And our Universities are now increasingly transformed into producers of engineers, just like IITs, while the University, which is by definition an incomparably higher educational institution, is precisely a place where closures of all onto-theological national humanisms are to be interrogated and questioned. This is the highest and greatest contribution that the University can make to the whole human race: that it must exceed, by its very axiomatic presence, all possible closures and hegemonic dominations. The University professor and the University student, by definition, occupy incomparably higher places among the human kind, in their very worldly destitution. In their very fragility, they bear a power that keeps the human race open to its radical and redemptive futurity.

'All that is Solid Melts into the Air'*

Dear "Professor" Vice-Chancellor,
Jawaharlal Nehru University, New Delhi

When the clamour is made all around us, and rightly so, about the condition of the growing degeneration of quality education in the higher institutions of learning in our country, you have justly—for which you must be praised—taken up the messianic responsibility, in a heroic manner, to rescue "quality education" from its shipwreck. How can a colleague, fortunate that one is to be your colleague, not praise you for your mission of life?: that is, to contribute to the social welfare, to the human resources of the nation (the third or second biggest democracy in the world), to make the already great university like JNU at par with the best universities in the world for which it

---

* Open letter to the VC of Jawaharlal Nehru University has been previously published in *Governance Now.*

is necessary, so you think, to raise the bar even higher (for your colleagues to be promoted to professor, for example, which is just one example among many).

These are all beautiful things, beautifully beautiful things to be realized, and thanks that you have spent the last one and a half years of your life in JNU in thinking and realizing these beautiful things that we see in your very being and very acts. Your colleagues and students, ungrateful and unthought that they are, have condemned you, filed many petitions in the court against you, but alas, nobody has publicly praised you, let alone calling you "Yog Purush" which you rightly deserve! However, I have a few brief remarks to make. Since you do not like to meet your colleagues nor am I being an authority like you to use up public taxpayers' money to spend on lawyers in the court, I have no other way but to take recourse to this open letter to you. I hope you will read this letter (since you have never replied to my official letters, I presume you have never read them).

I have known and been associated with this university for nearly two decades now, first as a student and then as a faculty, and I have never seen the university in such a degenerate condition as now. The question that is to be asked, which is the question par excellence, is: why now? Especially now when the administrative head of the institution heroically and messianically—with a team of worldly-wise intellectuals to support him—is trying to uplift it even higher to the sky (like the Tower of Babel?)?

This is the question you yourself, even more than anyone else, ought to be asking: why this university now, which was blooming with youthful energy of students and promising teachers—an oasis in our national life—suddenly has sunk, under your very leadership, into the graveyard of intellect? It is the fundamental question that neither you nor I, or anyone of this nation can evade responding to it: your uplifting, in just slightley more than one year's time, has shipwrecked this beautiful university which has otherwise helped flourish, in numerous ways, the spiritual-intellectual life of this country for decades. Everybody is shocked, aghast, and anguished at what is happening just in front of their eyes: an oasis turned to ruins, a beautiful garden suddenly demolished and made into the graveyard of intellect. You have been staying for long just on the opposite side of the university gate before you entered: have you not noticed this horrible site, so painful to bear, this site of ruins and graveyards with wreckages and garbage all piling up all around in the campus now in just more than a year? An institution takes decades, sometimes even a century, to be built up, and it takes just a year to turn it into a graveyard.

It is now a good time to ask you a question, the question that better be asked by yourself to yourself (since you do not ask yourself, I take this chance to ask you): is there something wrong in your messianism and heroism? Maybe it is not at all a messianism but precisely is its exact opposite?

Please do not misunderstand me. I do not regret that I am not promoted to be professor, despite knowing that you have found me unsuitable on a ground that does not exist in any rule book (neither in UGC notification nor in JNU Acts and Ordinances), and despite knowing that you have still promoted others who also have no such ground (you have promoted a faculty member who does not have any PhD supervision at the time of promotion). I am also not carrying any ill will against you despite knowing that this is completely unethical and unjust, and is a blatant and condemnable discrimination of me. But this irony is precisely the truth that gives us the horror: while a Dalit is soon going to be the President of India, another Dalit is discriminated against: it exhibits, more than ever before, that the millennium-long caste discrimination has now become very smart, so smart that even the President of the country is not spared! What to expect from you, dear "professor" Vice-Chancellor?

To return to the fundamental question: why is it that the little oasis in an immense country which was blooming only a short while ago, has suddenly turned itself into ruins? It is the question that neither I nor you can escape, for it concerns this entire country and beyond it. The life of a nation, without spirit and intellect, is no life but a cage or a factory (which is the same), for spirit is the foundation of life, and that is why, poets, philosophers and scholars are the inaugurators of history and are its consummate fullness. I understand that you, coming from an Electric Engineering background, will not understand these words that sound like jargon. But these words convey the very truth of the university: that by definition, by its very axiomatic presence, the university is universal in spirit, and can never serve the narrow interests of a parochial nationalism represented by a hegemonic regime. That is why it is absolutely essential that a scholar and intellectual—that yourself are as much as I am—be away from the princes of the world, from the powers that emanate from the hegemonic regimes at place.

Now this is precisely the answer to that fundamental question: by your very intimate association with the princes of the world, you have distorted the very messianic task that you have given yourself. It only shows that truth that is difficult to agree: the administrative head of the university does not know what the university is, and confuses it with an industry of mechanical (or electrical, if you like) knowledge production that serves the interests of the state from which the dominant class always profits. The task of the university is, unlike what you think as "industry" (this is your word), creative production of thinking that critically engages the fundamental questions of existence, whether social or individual, that go beyond the closures of hegemonic nationalism, and it is this critical thinking that keeps the very national life alive, open to its historical future, and nourishes its intellectual-existential foundation. This is the contribution of the university which the administrative head of the university must cultivate: the spirit of creative thinking that is irreducible to the technical apparatus of domination.

Unfortunately, you know absolutely nothing of this, absolutely nothing! Instead foregrounding this as your task and allow the university to grow even higher than where we are now, what we see right from the first page of our university website (where your photographs are everywhere), a factory in becoming, a big mechanical-bureaucratic apparatus of domination. I do not need to cite the examples of innumerable breaking of rules (the refusal of my promotion is just one of them) under your establishment, promoting extremely mediocre people while harassing and intimidating colleagues who are reputed for scholarly works, and everything else that is leading the university to its utter annihilation so much so that every day when I come to my office, it feels like a graveyard. All that is beautiful and solid, as Marx put it, has melted into the air! And for all this, the judgment is upon the self-proclaimed Messiah whose messianic task has gone all wrong. Instead of taking the university forward, your false messianism has taken the university at least a hundred years backward.

The Wolf and the Lamb*

At no other moment in the history of Indian national life after independence are the Dalits as oppressed as this moment: Dalits are set ablaze on the living fire, slaughtered like animals on the slaughtering bench of history, and humiliated like slaves in the marketplace in full daylight. When the social hierarchy is interiorized, and reduplicated within the institutionalized life of higher education like the university, it assumes the name 'meritocracy'.

The idea of merit that is based on the neoliberal logic of quantification, classification and control, through which the capital recharges itself, is now combined with the millennium-long social injustice based on caste discrimination. This is how in today's world of extreme capitalism where only the fittest survive in the life-and-

---

* Earlier published in *Governance Now*.

death struggle—and where the idea of merit serves as the paradigm of exclusion and elimination–the social injustice is intellectualised. The neoliberal world of extreme capitalism, thus, has not eliminated social injustice—for example, the caste hierarchy in India—but rather perpetuates it in ever new forms, of which the idea of merit is its latest avatar.

The reduction of knowledge to commodity production, like any other commodities that bear economic values in the world market, is blind and deaf to the burning and the absolute question of social justice. It reduces the question of social justice to an issue belonging to the field of conditioned negotiations in the realm of practical politics, while on the other hand, it upholds the idea of merit as a politically neutral one that serves the interest of any and each individual, provided that one has the merit and proves it. This supposed equality, which is actually a homogenization of singularities into quantitative entities, is, at the same instance—and this is its blind spot—perpetuation of social inequality.

This is, as it has always been, also the truth of the space called 'university life': the social injustice is being constantly subsumed and kept hidden—and thus perpetuated—under the supposedly neutral concept of 'merit', but the truth is precisely the opposite: the top of the hierarchy will almost always be occupied by not just the economically dominant class but the socially dominant caste. Through the mechanism of merit, the hegemonic apparatus subtly, in the most refined manner possible, keeps the lower castes at the lowest level possible, subjugating them in the most repressive manner, though in the light of day it does not appear so coercive.

Even in a university like Jawaharlal Nehru University, especially under the current establishment, the work of reduplicating the social hierarchy into the interiorized idea of merit is visible in the most glaring manner, and when this institutionally legitimated idea of merit does not work—when a faculty or a student, for example, is even better than other colleagues even in accordance to the paradigm of merit—coercive force is used by the legitimate authority in the most brutal, corrupt and rotten manner possible.

To cite an example: in my own case of promotion, through the 'Career Advancement Scheme' at JNU from 'associate professor' to 'professor', the present legitimate authority (who functions like a dictator) used his authority, in the most brutal manner possible, to stop my promotion even though I have fulfilled all academic qualifications. He invoked a criterion of promotion (that only he who has research scholars awarded a PhD under his supervision will be promoted) which exists neither in UGC nor in JNU rules. At the same time, he has misused his authority to promote another colleague who does not even have PhD scholars working with him.

It is a blatant example of caste discrimination that is possible even in a university like JNU. It only reminds us of the story of the wolf: when it no longer could argue with the little lamb who is drinking spring water downhill, the wolf argued that even if the little lamb did not pollute the water, his ancestors had done so. The wolf thereby took the liberty to punish the little lamb: it jumped on him and crushed him to death.

The caste discrimination, thus, takes an infinite number of forms, gestures, nuances and shades possible: when arguments work, then it is fine; when arguments do not work, then force and violence are to be used; in any case, social injustice has to be perpetuated, hegemonic domination has to be reproduced, for reproduction of the condition of production—as the philosopher Louis Althusser insightfully explains—is the very logic of hegemonic domination. The caste question as part of the university curriculum, within the closed doors of the classroom, is all that is fine, but the instance it breaks out and wants to transform the social situation, and puts into question unspeakable and barbaric violence of hegemonic forces, then every weapon must be used to stop it.

It is extremely difficult for a Dalit to be professor where the caste discrimination rules in such a manner, even though the Dalit faculty member has achieved excellence, in so many different ways, in his academic work. The logic of merit is used precisely to stop any Dalit colleagues to rise in the professional space, and when even this does not work, then the most corrupt ways will be used to stop the Dalits. Here, as elsewhere, the Brahminical order is governed by what Friedrich Nietzsche calls 'resentment': the illogical logic through which social injustice and social inequality are legitimated and justified is the logic that the wolf gives. And the wolf is full of resentment.

The question of social justice is the absolute and unconditional question. It concerns the very foundation of the historical existence of the Indian nation. No one can evade it by reducing it to a conditioned fulfilment through practical politics. It demands the complete revolutionizing of the Indian society at large.

Destruction of the University*

The recent remark of the Vice-Chancellor of Jawaharlal Nehru University that he desires to install a tank in the University campus to instil our love for the country has made this absolutely clear: that the VC has absolutely no interest in the University, and therefore, he has no moral right to remain in the University, if not for any other than for the simple reason is that he has gone absolutely muddleheaded, and confused, in the broad daylight of the day, between the University space and the battlefield. To substantiate his confusion, he invites a cricketer and an army officer to a University (to a University) who speak of military style conquest of the Universities of the country, of which JNU is the topmost name. This event is absolutely unprecedented: in no good University in the entire world—"University" worthy of its name—have

---

* Earlier published in *Indian Cultural Forum*.

army officers and the VCs ever spoken of conquering the space of the University by using military force and brutal political power. Meanwhile the University is just breathing its last, and barely surviving on its ruin: there is no book in the library; students live in the hostel in the most unhygienic and unbearable conditions possible; there is absolutely no fund for higher research, especially in the social sciences and humanities; there is hardly any good facility in the University that are basic, like healthcare, etc; many students, coming from distant places, do not have hostel room; meanwhile, there is a drastic seat cut, and hardly any admission in any of the research programmes. All avenues of peaceful protests, which is the only thing University teachers and students can do, are punished in the most brutal and savage manner possible. Meanwhile there is the absolutism of corruption at all possible levels (faculty recruitment, faculty promotion, dealing with students and teachers, fabrication of lies and doctored videos, intimidation and threats to University professors, promoting the most mediocre and corrupt people who support the administration, etc) and dictatorship in all its horror and tyranny: all rules which do not serve the interest of the establishment are discarded in the dustbins, while rules are fabricated every day to deny, in the most repressive and coercive manner possible, any remote possibility of justice; functioning of all decision-making bodies of the University is now defunct and virtually does not exist; all decisions arrive from top to bottom, from the

VC to the rest, just in a military dictatorship and tyranny; anything remotely resembling democracy has now been abandoned; the basic rights of the employee are thrown into the dustbin (anybody can be kicked out anytime of his/her job for speaking critically about the establishment); the fundamental rights of the citizen—like freedom of speech—are violated; the constitutional rights, especially given to the deprived communities, are violated.

Undoubtedly the current VC has immense admiration for the military. The military dictatorship is his great paradigm, and he has modelled his own life, right from learning martial arts, on this pattern. It is this that interests the military VC of this University, and nothing, absolutely nothing in what the University needs: the VC absolutely does not care about the welfare and upliftment of the University, about academic excellence and promotion of higher researches, about inculcating the intellectual passion in the young minds, and enthusiastically participating, with his colleagues in the University, in the creative exercise of academic freedom. The VC of the University does not even meet his students and his colleagues, apart from his favourite ones, for his time is occupied with twittering and organizing events that please the ruling regime. In just one year's time an excellent University, only one of its kind in the country, has been ruined and yet the whole country looks on, helplessly, many of them blaming these students who are excellent researchers in the University for misusing tax payers' money.

A University is the singular and unique institution in a national life: even though established in the geographical territory of a specific nation, the University yet exceeds closures of all forms of nationalism. As its very name 'University' suggests, there is something universal about University: everything under the sun can be researched upon, critically discussed and interrogated, venturing beyond all ethnic-national-geographical boundaries and closures, passing all geographical-political boundaries *sans papier*. That is why, the University is the philosophical institution par excellence, and since it is the philosophical institution, every higher degree (Master of Philosophy, Doctor of Philosophy, etc.) given by the University is the philosophical degree, even though one may not have done research exclusively and strictly on philosophy. It is not for nothing that the very idea and the institution of 'the academy' is the invention of a philosopher, namely Plato. In this profound sense, all those who are in the University, including the VC, are philosophers, and not military people. Therefore, it is a downright insult to the very venerable institution called the University when the VC requests a tank to be installed in the campus, and it is a downright betrayal of his own profession as the administrative leader of the University community, as deplorable as the police stealing like thieves, and as those who are supposed to be apostles reveal themselves to be only robbers.

The militarization of the University must be condemned, not only by all the professors and students across the country, but even by the country citizens and those who are in the honourable profession of the military who must protect us, not only from external enemies, but abusing the military power by an academic head. The excess and the ecstasy of the University, beyond all forms of national closures, has neither anything nationalist nor anything anti-national about it: it is the very spiritual fecundity of the University space that, by putting into question all nationalist closures, enriches and fructifies the spiritual life of the nation. To destroy the paradox is to destroy the very fecundity and the spiritual life of the University, and thus, of the very spiritual life of the nation. This is why any coercive or ideological repression of academic-intellectual freedom of the University is the most anti-national sentiment ever.

Therefore, all the great Universities in the world, some of them are a thousand years old, are nourished even by the respective nationalist regimes. The University is the institution that singularly keeps the spiritual foundation, not just of the respective nation, but of humanity alive. That is why we can say that scholars, intellectuals and academics are the true inaugurators of history and of our political existence. To repress the University is the treason against which we must unanimously condemn, not only as 'anti-nationalist' but 'anti-humanity'. What the military dictatorship in JNU wants from us is silent, thoughtless, uncritical and unquestioning acceptance of the ruling regime which wards off all possible futurity of the nation and the university. And this is precisely what the University is supposed to question, discuss, and interrogate.

What is in a Name?*

At those certain historical moments when names too lofty for a phenomenon (names that conceal and manifest the phenomenon at the same time) have once more shown themselves to be decadent and demeaning, then it becomes imperative to invent a new name. When names like 'harijan', in their very loftiness and sublimity once more came to conceal the utterly lacerated existence of the untouchables in India, it was imperative to invent a new name 'Dalit'. Thus, the event of the name—the name 'Dalit' here—is born out of a paradox, and responds to this paradox: the too lofty name 'harijan' is too demeaning and humiliating to indicate the humiliated condition of the oppressed ones! The sublime word or the name 'harijan'—the people of God—does not reflect the scattered, bruised, wounded and lacerated condition of the untouchables;

* Earlier published in *The Beacon*.

in a cunning way, this idolization masks the real, brutal condition of an epochal suffering of millennium long. The name here becomes idolatry.

The name 'Dalit', then, is intended to disclose the idolatry of all hegemonic oppression that the regime in force perpetuates. For reproduction of its domination, the hegemonic force never ceases producing and reproducing phantasms that emanate from idols: in the words of the French philosopher Louis Althusser, they 'interpellate' the whole ideological apparatus, and in this manner, masks its true character. The subjects, thus interpellated, then 'interiorize' the hegemonic domination which makes reproduction of domination easier and less coercive. This explains how in a patriarchal society women can become the very agents of oppression against other women, and in a millennium-long caste-based society, Dalits may accept the hegemonic domination as something 'natural' and 'essential'. What is non-natural is naturalized and essentialized, concealing the historical character of these phenomena, as if women are naturally and essentially inferior, as if Dalits are naturally and essentially inferior, socially as much as individually, morally as much as physically. In names like 'harijan', which are supposed to elevate the inhumane condition of the Dalits, end up producing phantasms; by taking away the flesh and blood from women, they are now turned into goddesses, into fantastic figures which do not know any human suffering of real flesh and blood of women.

What, then, is in a name can only be understood by posing the question: who is naming it? In each act of naming by the hegemonic force, there is originary violence: it wants to exhaust the infinity of the phenomenon (the unspeakable and unnameable sufferings of the Dalits) in the name. The name becomes a classifiable category in the administrative order of things which can be manipulated, managed, ordered by bureaucratic and political reason. The name, then, becomes an item that signifies a group of numbered people (and statistics of demographic census helps) which ends up becoming a 'vote bank' to fight for elections. The absolute and non-negotiable, the measureless and nameless sufferings of certain people are now reduced to a manipulable group which can be administered in sight of conditioned and negotiable rights through constitutional means. It conveniently forgets the whole absolute and unconditional demands of absolute justice. The very name, which is supposed to elevate the lacerated condition of a certain people, has become a mere political means of perpetual political hegemony of the dominant caste.

Therefore, it is absolutely imperative to inquire who is naming whom? There is violence in imposing a name, a cognitive violence, which is the ground of all possible political and administrative violence of the hegemonic power. The colonial power which came to India and ruled over us for more than a hundred years knew the power of the name. It does not have to be a linguistic name: a flag, an anthem, a symbol, a spectacle can do the same. The event of naming (a street, a library, a University, etc.) is, therefore, not neutral: when used by the hegemonic force, the name 'harijan' becomes idolatry, a phantasm, a myth.

Therefore, the name 'Dalit' became necessary at certain historical moments in India. Sounding almost like an 'onamonapia', it is to evoke, not what is nameable, calculable and categorial but something like infinity of a bruised existence which is unnameable and immeasurable, beyond all totality and totalizable historical experience that is subsumed under the gaze of administrative and political reason. Instead of fixing the phenomenon called 'untouchable', the name 'Dalit' is intended to open up the whole world of naturalization and essentialization on whose basis the hegemonic force operates and legitimates itself. Such a name 'Dalit' can, then, only be provisional: once the hegemonic force withers away, and social justice prevails, the name 'Dalit' too will one day wither away. The name 'Dalit' does not, therefore, signify a natural entity, but an immense and measureless human suffering which is historically produced by the Brahminical order. As a historical product, along with the withering away of the hegemonic force, the name too will wither away.

The subject of this withering cannot be the hegemonic force. From Hegel and Marx we know that the subject of radical historical transformation has never been and is never the hegemonic force, but the subject that is oppressed, wounded, scattered and bruised in human civilization.

This is the privilege, not of the Brahminical order, but that of the Dalits: it is the Dalits and it is women who are the real subjects of radical transformation of human history. By being the very minus figures in human history, they bring about historical transformations which are incalculable and revolutionary. The hegemonic force, on the other hand, suppresses such transformations, calling them back to the order which helps perpetuate their domination in turn.

What is, then, in a name? What is in the name 'Dalit'? We can say: 'everything' and 'nothing'. The name 'Dalit' does not mean anything particular (localizable, datable, manipulable and manageable entity in service of the administrative reason), but for that matter it is not a mere nothing: it opens up the demand of absolute, non-negotiable and unconditional social justice that cannot be reduced to political-practical negotiations through constitutional means by winning elections. In other words, it begs the immense question of the ethical that exceeds the conditioned politics of negotiable demands and rights.

The Truth is Always Persecuted*

I. The Decision of Existence

Sometimes, suddenly in our life, we encounter the moment of decision that we cannot evade: either we become slavishly complicit with the princes of the world, wash their feet, and get petty morsels of worldly benefits that fall from their table; or, we are ready to give up, if necessary, many worldly benefits, but, retain our absolute fidelity to truth, to one's own conscience, knowing that truth is always persecuted. Where should we go: towards the narrow and straight way; or, towards the wide way where crowds and multitudes throng, the road where everything we see is crooked? Every great decision is

---

* Earlier published published in *Guftugu*.

always *either/ or*– as Søren Kierkegaard says—and there is no middle path. In fact, the middle path is the great illusion of the petty bourgeoisie. There are only two ways in life, for every third or fourth way is still only the second way; for truth is always the singular and irreducible. It can only be a one-way street.

This is the essence of tragic thought: the thought of the two in their incommensuration; there is no dialectical third to totalize and include this disparate within it. To live tragically, is to live at the extreme limit of thought where decision occurs out of the abyss of freedom. Not deciding, that is, not assuming freedom too, comes already out of the abyss of an inscrutable freedom. In a certain way, we are already decided, and we have already decided what we are. This essential decision is already the decision of existence itself, out of the abyssal freedom. The only thing is to follow the decision of existence to its limit, and then see what happens there.

What erupts, out of this decision, is nothing less than the radical demand of the unconditional. One may call it truth or justice. This unconditional demand can never be arrived at in a calculable process of conditioned negotiations of practical politics. To discuss with the other party in a roundtable style approach, where each one plays his/her card, and to see how much each one is prepared to negotiate to arrive at the conditioned solution of mutually negotiable demands: this is the gravest illusion of the secular parliamentary democracies. It does not know anything of the unconditioned demand of life, of justice and truth. It flattens out everything into the conditioned politics of practical negotiations.

Thought tragically, there is, then, a limit of dialogue. For example, what is there to conduct a dialogue with an establishment that has replaced all speech with horror, where every word is a murder, where every sentence is an annihilation of humanity? All talk of 'reformation' – which any of the established regime always evokes—that only maintains the homogeneity and continuum of the evolutionary scale, where only the fittest survive after a struggle of life and death: all such talk is sheer complicity from the perspective of the vanquished, and those who are oppressed by history. Their claim of justice is so absolute that only the unconditioned satisfies them; the rest is only untruth and a betrayal of the truth.

II. The Infinite Contestation

The tragic decision demands an infinite contestation: not the contestation of one hegemonic regime trying to establish another regime to come, but infinite contestation of any and each hegemonic regime in one place, at any point of time. The tragic thought, thus, introduces the thought of death into politics: in operation of any hegemonic regime, phantasm destitutes the regime that it anchors. We must be able to find out, with infinite vigilance, the phantasm that operates, supports and anchors the hegemonic regime; then uproot it from its ground, and exhibit it as what it really is: a mere phantasm and not truth, a mere myth and not history. For all hegemonic regimes are mythically founded; in other words, it is based on a fiction or a phantasm, whether it is the racist Aryan identity for the Nazis, or communism for Stalin, or our very own Aryan nationalism. The tragic thought must pierce through the mythic phantasm of the political regime at place and unravel, interrupt and de-constitute the law of its being. It is poetry, art and philosophy that bear that cry which pierces through the murderous speech of the hegemonic regime. This is why art and philosophy are the highest activities of the human race. This is why every hegemonic regime would either wish to appropriate and domesticate the artist, the philosopher and the writer; or, it would like to banish them from the regime. In any case, the poet, the philosopher and the artist, are inhospitable to the constituted order of the political regime; by their mere presence and by their mere insubordination they exhibit the truth that is indigestible and an inhospitable remainder of the world. This is the paradox par excellence: by their very being at the limit of the world, they salvage the world from the shipwreck of humanity.

Only infinite contestation, already opened by an opening of pure affirmation, can keep our world open to the futurity to arrive. It is poetry, art and philosophy, emerging from the depth of the dark earth that keeps the promise of the new future for humanity alive. When everything is said and done, and at whatever stage of progress or regress humanity finds itself, it is this promise alone that remains fruitful, the promise and the truth are always wounded and persecuted in the world. That is why, each time, we need to rescue it from hegemonic regimes through an infinite contestation.

III. Hic et Nunc

The infinite contestation must be unleashed each time, infinitely, here and now, especially today, and at this precise place more than ever before. When the destruction of the life of the spirit is nearly complete (the destruction of the University life in this country, under the regime at place, is only one example among many), when 'the document of barbarism' (Walter Benjamin) behind the glorious civilization called India is now revealed to us in the broad daylight of history in all its ugliness and horror; it is precisely here and now that we need to unleash the infinite contestation in its purity and infinity.

The space of the University is not one space among many of a national life. It is the very space, the only remaining space in today's world, which conserves and preserves the life of the spirit. It is out of this space alone, in today's world of advance capitalism, of mass consumption, that the spirit can unleash the infinite contestation in the name of purest affirmation. By infinitely interrogating the hegemonic regime which constantly serves the interest of the dominant class/caste/gender, the community of teachers and students within and outside the space of the University affirms a form of life freed from the cages of the law; a life liberated from the bondage of any oppression.

This is why the hegemonic regime and its intellectual servants have recently made attempts to depoliticize the space of the University, and purge any elements of the spirit of questioning and thinking. These attempts of the conservative regime to de-politicize education mean nothing other than the following: that we should accept their domination without critique, subversions, deconstructions and resistances. It is not for nothing that the dominant regime—this one at place particularly—always prefers technological education which is supposed to be politically neutral. The truth is that, technology is never politically neutral: not only are the technologists and scientists often, politically and socially, the most regressive ones, but technological domination has always gone hand in hand with political and social domination. Therefore, it is not surprising that our pseudo-mystics who revive some obscurantist elements of Hindu mysticism, often eulogize technological power. By selling us the cheap idea of technological progress, the mystics of political authority want us to also buy their authority and domination in the name of progress. We can find the secret of this nexus here. This nexus constitutes the mystic foundation of political authority. All legitimacy-seeking authority evokes myth as the very foundation of political domination.

Hic et nunc! Here and now, the decision of existence must be reached on the basis of the immeasurable of either/or, and it is only from within this space called the University, where such decision may erupt and upsurge: the decisions to say 'no' to any oppression and domination, and the refusal to accept injustice, in the name of an absolute justice or truth. Such form of life that we call here the 'spiritual life', cultivated within the space called the University, is not the life of fragile beauty untouched by death and sacrifices, but the tragic life par excellence that never ceases to declare, even at the instance of death, that immortal 'No!'. And here, too, we know how truth is always persecuted. This declarative speech 'No!' is, however, only another way of saying 'Yes' to the absolute justice which is not yet but soon to come, yet coming, just after a short while.

The Withering Away of the University*

The series of events that have unfolded, and are still unfolding, at one of the premier institutions of higher education and research of this country, that is, Jawaharlal Nehru University, is symptomatic of a deep-seated, mostly unconscious, malaise. From far, or from distance it appears that it is the internal conflict between two opposing political ideologies—"left" and "right"—seeking domination, and in fact, this is precisely the appearance that a certain group is invested, not without reason, to proclaim. A closer look should reveal the real truth: that this "appearance" is a fiction which is invested with the value of "truth", and that it is propagated by those who are apologetic of the current administrative apparatus. And it is not difficult to see why.

---

* Earlier published in *Indian Cultural Forum*.

The question is not really the internal battle between "left and "right", though it is true that those few faculty members who support "the regime" at place can be said to be more or less of the conservative disposition, while the immense number of students and teachers on the other side (the overwhelming number is demonstrated each time in all those massive events of protests that have occurred in the last two years) are not necessarily the supporter of any "left" political ideology or of a party. The real question, which is obscured in all those heated debates that have taken place in the last two years, is rather this: an immense number of students and teachers of this University are attempting to preserve the very ethos of, not only this University, but of what University *as such* by definition is, and ought to be: a place of intellectual and spiritual freedom, freedom from the hegemonic regime at place (whatever that regime may be at any instance of time, left or right), freedom from all external coercion to pursue, fearlessly, what is beneficial to the interests of the Universe as such (that is why it is called "University") and of humanity at large, beyond all closures of the nation, race, community, religion or sexuality. The state and the administration are those facilitating agents to foster knowledge and wisdom of the highest order that flourish in this spiritual site; the state and the administration are responsible for this nourishment of critical thinking and intellectual freedom: in this sense, the state and the administration are obliged—if not by the force of the law, but at least ethically (therefore, this obligation is even higher than any legal obligation)—to the protection and nourishment of the University as such.

What we see in the last few decades is the transformation of the role of the state in relation to the country at large. The state now no longer wants to see itself as a "social welfare" state, but as one multinational company among others, albeit bigger one than most of the other companies. With this transformation, the responsibility of the state to the social welfare is also fast disappearing: the state now wants to enter the vast, global market of profit-making business partnership with other countries through facilitating free market and privatization of almost every mode of our existence (including healthcare and transport) while using up the tax payer's money. In this process not only is the question of "social justice" (to the deprived sections, to the Dalits and minorities) considered redundant, the very space of University is also becoming a useless institution for the profit-making state, unless the University itself becomes somehow another profit-making institution, a factory or industry among others. When the University is reduced to a profit-making institution, the question of intellectual freedom and critical-creative transformation of humanity does not occur; instead, the real stake is how much profit the University is making. The decisive 55 per cent budget cut to UGC is only one symptom among others: there are massive seat cuts in almost all government-funded central universities of the country; a vast number of faculty is working on an ad hoc basis without any hope of recruitment in any near future; fellowships to research scholars in the Humanities and Social sciences are more or less either reduced or stopped altogether; even in a University like JNU, reservation policies in students' intake are not followed in the last two years, and thereby putting to shame the constitutional norms and rules that seek to establish social justice and equality. Very soon, this process of privatization of education will reach such magnitude that most of the young people of the coming generation of this country will be deprived of higher education and research altogether, not to mention the alarming phenomenon of unemployment that has already made itself felt.

What is happening here? What is happening at JNU is only symptomatic of what is happening in all institutions of higher education and research of this country: like the state which has forgotten its role as "social welfare" state, and instead has become a player in the marketplace of the capital accumulation (and thereby destroying the very idea of social justice, social equality, and upliftment of the well-being of the citizens), so the administrations of the Universities—and JNU is the prime example here—have to become players in the free market where knowledge is a commodity, students and teachers are mindless cogs in the immense apparatus of knowledge production who, by definition, must be deprived of any intellectual freedom to debate, to think, to examine matters of prime concern, not only of the nation but of the entire humanity. It is not for nothing that the current Vice-Chancellor of JNU speaks not only of battle tanks but also of "industry": this latter idea is far more sinister than the former. For him, this University is a laboratory and a factory which will produce commodities in the marketplace of the world; the University, for him, is a multinational company within the big multinational company of the nation. The administrator now no longer thinks himself as the facilitator of intellectual freedom and social justice, but as the engineer of profit in the marketplace of the world.

The paradoxical fact is that—in fact it is not at all a paradox—this very "neo-liberal" economic theology is now combined with the most obscurantist and the most regressive, which is at once most dangerous and terrifying, political view to the society at large. The current administration happily combines the "neoliberal" economic theology (supported by the most sophisticated and advanced technological apparatus) with the most regressive and socially unjust cultural standpoint of extreme conservatism. At JNU currently, the flag of RSS happily flies with the flag of neo-liberal world-politics. What, then, is destroyed is the very place of an excellent University that for decades has contributed to the intellectual life, not only of the nation but to the world of learning as such. What, then, is destroyed is the very ethos of democracy and intellectual freedom, the very passion of critical thinking and creativity which flourished at this

University for the last so many decades.

One is tempted to say that what could not happen, to such an extent, at the level of national politics, has now happened in JNU: the rise of the absolute state; the merciless dictatorship of the VC at JNU which is supported by a few other profiteers; the taking place of the regime of terror where dissenting students and teachers are daily harassed, punished and humiliated; the taking place of a machinery of surveillance, of discipline and punishment. The question of attendance, which has recently raised such a huge uproar among students and teachers alike, is not one question among others: it is precisely the protest against the regime of terror at place today at JNU where everyone is terrorized; it is one desperate attempt, on the part of the students and teachers, to salvage the University from its headlong rush into the abyss of annihilation. Not to mention corruption: all possible norms, rules, laws—of the University and the law of the land—are thrown into the dustbins. What once resonated: "Hail, intellectual freedom!", now appears: "Hail, our leader VC."

It is the responsibility of the nation to protect and nourish its intellectual and spiritual institutions. What is going on at the University currently is neither a sectarian fight of a sect for some tangible privileges and benefits, nor even political domination for a "left" ideology, but a painful, bitter, difficult struggle to preserve a precious institution of an entire nation from the forces of destruction.

Infinite Contestation*

At the heart of the phenomenon of the Sahitya Akademi Award winning writers returning their awards, one that has been the subject of much heated discussions in the last few days, at the heart of these events lies the following question: how to think of responsibility today, a responsibility that is inextricably bound up with the question of the possibility of contestation, and, concomitantly, the very possibility of *the political* for writers, intellectuals, artists etc.

The question of *the political* has constantly been submerged repeatedly in the chaos of voices that rise so loud that the essential and truly decisive question cannot be posed. It thus appears that *the political* at stake for these writers and artists, *the political* in the name of which these writers are voicing their protest or contesting,

---

* Earlier published in *Café Dissensus.*

is somehow not commensurable with what professional politicians (this includes professional intellectuals, those intellectual apologists of given and dominant hegemonic regimes) mean by "politics". It is an imperative and a responsibility now, more than ever before (that means "urgently" and "immediately"), to bring forth to visibility, to manifestation, this anathema or this "scandal" that lies in the hiatus between *the political* in the name of which an infinite contestation is being carried out by intellectuals and artists, and, on the other hand, the politics of conditioned negotiations and transactions between powers, forces and gazes.

This appeared in an exemplary mode, like a flash of lightning only to disappear again, immediately, in the vast sky of darkness, in one of the countless debates in one of the English news channels recently. Three writers and artists of repute who have returned their awards were invited along with a professional intellectual of a certain political party to comment and discuss the Union Minster's trashing "comment" that this is an unjustified thing for intellectuals to do, a thing which is nothing more than a "paper rebellion", a "manufactured crisis" for the Prime Minister, an impotent attempt without much consequence.

The Union Minister explains the phenomenon in the following way: those intellectuals and artists are now at odds with the current regime; they are those who enjoyed the patronage of the previous regime but are no longer pampered. As such, this phenomenon is none other than an irrational resentment, this whole "paper rebellion"; a bad politics, a "politics by other means", which means, "means" without "means". As if, there is something essentially bad about "paper" (this "paper rebellion"), for it constantly refuses to use force or power, and yet constantly, that means hypocritically, it accepts to be benefited by (another) power and (another) force, which for the Union Minster is the other political party, which itself is now constantly mobilizing forces to return to power once again.

What is symptomatic—and this is important for any good diagnosis—of this Minister's trashing comment, and subsequently of the professional intellectual at the service of the dominant regime in the debate, is the refusal to understand that the infinite contestation, wherein lies the true political and true responsibility, that the writers and artists "symbolically" (that is without force, without power, without gaze) carry out their resistance, cannot be reduced to the conditioned politics of negotiations between forces, powers and gazes. That means, the infinite contestation must constantly open the realm of conditionality of politics to something unconditional, to something like *justice*, which infinitely and always overflows, exceeds, surpasses any given (whether right or left or centric; whether conservative, radical or liberal) regime of political power at any given historical juncture.

Herein lies the aporia of responsibility, which is the very aporia of the political, for writers and intellectuals: whether understood from the perspective of a political regime that has forces at its disposal to legitimize its hegemony (and it is all "democratic", as if democracy is automatically self-legitimate) or from the perspective of a political regime that may come into dominance some time later but now has been dethroned from dominance, there is politics only in this sense: "if you don't support me or if you criticize me, that means you are on the other side". This concept of politics is totalizing; it is exhausted in determination of it as conditioned negotiations between forces, powers and gazes.

A non-subscription to this politics is considered to be even worse: a writer is irresponsible (because she supports neither me nor my enemy), apolitical (she refuses to contest power in the name of power, force in the name of force, violence in the name of violence), and even worse, is an opportunist. And yet, thought carefully and responsibly, in this irresponsibility lies the highest responsibility for writers and artists; in this apolitics lies a higher political. The political irresponsibility is apolitics and yet political in a profounder sense: this aporia cannot be understood by one who either has legitimized forces at its disposal or who is working towards such legitimacy. In that sense, the responsibly irresponsible metapolitics of writers has nothing to do with legitimation; it is rather infinite delegitimation of any given worldly powers at any given historical point, and hence its contestation is infinite: it does not rest satisfied with juxtaposing one power against another power, or privileging one force against another force.

Therefore, writing and creating works of art or pursuing truth in philosophy, all these fragile things that they do—fragile because they do not have forces at their disposal—this fragility is excessive: they overflow, like a surplus, the entire forceful and powerful realm of politics. That this apolitical politics, or this political or metapolitics is a good thing is seen in the precise way in which the dominant powerful regimes feel attacked. Here is the enigma of the work of art: in its powerlessness, it opens up something like an infinite justice, not yet actualized in any worldly regimes of power, which makes power—despite its measureless appearance—limited or finite. This disinvestment or this withdrawing of stakes from any given worldly regimes that constantly need from us normative obligations, this rebellion is apolitics and political at the same time.

It is the task of the intellectuals, writers and artists to be irresponsible in the name of this infinite responsibility: that is, in creating works of art, and pursing truth to show this yawning abyss, itself a fragile abyss, between politics and the political, between law and justice, between force and truth, between power and peace, and to allow forces to confront this abyss wherein they are paralyzed, dazed and transfixed.